Ashley

I hope you enjoy this book. It's been fun having you here. May <u>God</u> continue to bless you

Love Julia Kim

DEC. '99

Presented to:

Julia Kim

Date:

Dec. 23,

THE TEN COMMANDS

FROM GOD'S OWN HANDS

Ten wiggly, giggly Bible stories
that teach God's Ten Commandments

Written & Illustrated by
Phil A. Smouse

Chariot Victor Publishing
A Division of Cook Communications

For Annette, Danielle, and Davey

Lord, let this be the generation to bring your commandments
of love back into the homes and hearts of men.
Matthew 22:36-40

Published by Chariot Family Publishing, a division of Cook Communications,
Colorado Springs, Colorado.

ISBN 0-7814-3259-6

Printed in the United States of America

1 2 3 4 5 6 7 — 02 01 00 99

THE TEN

1. I AM THE LORD YOUR GOD...YOU SHALL HAVE NO OTHER GODS BEFORE ME.
2. YOU SHALL NOT MAKE FOR YOURSELF AN IDOL.
3. YOU SHALL NOT MISUSE THE NAME OF THE LORD.
4. REMEMBER THE SABBATH DAY BY KEEPING IT HOLY.
5. HONOR YOUR FATHER AND YOUR MOTHER.

COMMANDMENTS

6. YOU SHALL NOT MURDER.
7. YOU SHALL NOT COMMIT ADULTERY.
8. YOU SHALL NOT STEAL.
9. YOU SHALL NOT GIVE FALSE TESTIMONY AGAINST YOUR NEIGHBOR.
10. YOU SHALL NOT COVET...ANYTHING THAT BELONGS TO YOUR NEIGHBOR.

CONTENTS

1. ADAM AND EVE 10
2. THE FIERY FURNACE 24
3. DAVID AND GOLIATH 40
4. THE CREATION STORY 56
5. ABRAHAM AND ISAAC 70
6. MY BROTHER'S KEEPER 80
7. JOSEPH AND POTIPHAR'S WIFE 92
8. THE WALLS OF JERICHO 104
9. DANIEL IN THE LION'S DEN 114
10. JOSEPH'S BEAUTIFUL COAT 130

WHAT ARE THE TEN COMMANDMENTS?

Do you ever wonder if God really loves you? Do you wonder if He is mad at you because of your mistakes? Well, God *does* love you. And He loves to give you good things. But He also knows that some things can hurt you.

Because God truly loves you, He wants what's best for you. He especially wants you to be able to know right from wrong.

So, many years ago, God spoke with a man named Moses. Moses trusted God and believed what He said. God gave Moses ten good rules. With these rules, God's children would always be able to know right from wrong. We call these rules God's Ten Commandments.

But these are not ordinary rules - oh no! There's something very strange about these Ten Commandments.

The harder you try to keep them, the more difficult they become to keep! In fact, God's rules are so hard to keep that *no one* has ever been able to keep them. Everyone has broken God's rules.

But that is a GOOD thing!

What!? How can *that* be good?

VISIT BEAUTIFUL
Mt.
SINAI

You see, our inability to obey God's Ten Commandments points out our deep need for God *Himself.*

Because we have all broken God's laws, God sent His Son Jesus to the Earth. When Jesus died on the cross, He took the punishment we deserved for breaking Gods rules!

When I accept what Jesus did on the cross, and believe that God raised Him from the dead, God forgives me for breaking His rules!

But where is Jesus now? Jesus wants to live inside of me. And just as He did long ago, Jesus will come from heaven - He will come right now - and live inside of my heart. All I have to do is ask.

When Jesus lives inside of my heart, I can learn to love God. I can even learn to love other people - not just say I love them, but *really* love them - the way Jesus loves me. That's what God's Ten Commandments are all about.

THE STORY OF ADAM AND EVE
GENESIS 2:4 - 3:24

By the sound of His voice, in the still of the night,
long before the first whisper of darkness or light,
On a wee-tiny, shiny, blue ball out in space
God began an amazing, mysterious place.

For with hands never heard and with eyes never seen,
God created a garden so silent and green.
Then He filled it with things that hum, bubble, and buzz -
full of all that there is, ever would be, or was!

But something was missing - some *one* or some *who*...
and so God reached down into the muck and the goo.
And there, from a handful of soggy, wet sod -
from a squishy, wet, wee, water-loggy, brown clod,

From the dust and the dirt - from the muck and the clay,
God created the very first man on that day!

And that man whom God made out of dirt and debris, yes, that made out of muddy, brown muck man is *me!*

And God breathed and said, *"ADAM!"* And POW! - I arose, then He wound up my mind and untangled my toes And said, *"Whip out your clippers and haul out your hose-- go take care of my garden and see that it grows."*

So I watered the lilies. I fluffed up the flowers.
I patted the bunnies for hours and hours.

But, oh I was lonely as lonely can be.
not one flounder or flea was as lonely as me!
For as I often say, and as everyone knows,
every guy needs a girl everywhere that he goes.

So one night while I snurgled, all snug in my bed,
and as visions of flounder lips danced in my head,
God snuck up and plucked one of the ribs from my side...

and He made me my very own beautiful bride!

Well, I looked at that girl and my heart went ker-thump,
my poor throat crimped and crinkled up into a lump.
But I reached out my hand. and she reached hers out too…
it was love at first yab-a-dab, dab dabba-doo!

And right there in the night, we embraced - and we kissed,
then we *both* heard God's voice…

We both heard Him say THIS:

"I AM GOD! I am ONE! *I AM Faithful and True!*
I made all of this stuff just for you and for you!
You may fill up your tummies with gladness and glee
with the yummy, good fruit found on any old tree.

But *whatever* you hear and whatever you do,
you must NEVER, not EVER, chomp, nibble, or chew,
You must NEVER gulp, gobble, nip, nubble, or gnaw
on the juicy, pink fruit of THIS tree - THAT'S THE LAW!

If you eat from *this* tree - if you dare to, or try,
on the day that you do, you will both surely DIE!"

So we did what God said. Yes, we did what we should,
because God was our God, and oh boy, was God good!
And we'd giggle and play *every* night and each day...

'Til we met up with old "you-know-who," as they say!

He slid down from that tree with a thlippery *thump*,
then he curled up his rump in a leathery lump.
And he slithered right up to my sweet, little wife.
And with five little words he just *ruined* our life!

"Now, did God *really* say," hissed that slobbery slug,
"'you must never gulp, glibble, glurp, globble, or glug,
From the yummy, pink fruit found on every good tree
in *my* beautiful Garden of Eden.' Did He?

That's a joke! It's a trick! It's a fib - it's a LIE!
GO AHEAD - EAT THE FRUIT ... *You WILL NOT surely die!*"

Well, Eve looked at the fruit, and you know it looked good!
And for one tiny second she thought that she could
just go right on ahead and just do her own thing -
As if God wasn't there - as if God didn't care,
as if God wasn't God every day, *everywhere!*

So she *DID* it! *She ate it!* Then I ate it too
and the very next half a split-second we knew...

Oh, I looked up at Eve and then Eve looked at me,
and Eve started to scream, and I started to flee!
For I noticed her toe, then she noticed my knee,
so she jumped in a bush, and I ran up a tree!

And right then and right there as we quivered and quaked,
we both knew we'd been *tricked* by that sneaky old snake!
But we did what we did and *we knew it was wrong,*
and we knew that GOD knew, and it wouldn't be long
'til we'd both have to face Him. And face Him we would.
And we knew He'd remove us from Eden for good!

And that's just what He did. *But we gave Him no choice.*
For WE made the mistake. We rejected His voice.

THE DEVIL'S A LIAR. *He always will be!*

So *whatever* you hear and *whatever* you do,
and whatever that snake tries to get you to do,
please remember God's love - and remember *our sin...*

THERE IS ONLY ONE GOD. Listen only to HIM!

God's first Commandment is:
1. I AM THE LORD

2. You shall not make for yourself an idol.

THE FIERY FURNACE

DANIEL 3:1-30

Now, some kings are okay. And some kings are all right,
and some kings do some things better kept out of sight.
Oh, but now and again, though you fiddle and futz,
you wind up with a king who's just chock-full of nuts!

And King Nebuchadnezzar - *"King Nebooka-WHOODLE?"*
King *NEB*, with the soft, goo-gum chewy, numb noodle!
He was wacky and nutty, and as you shall see,
his toot-fruity decree caused a major *"hooo-wheee!"*

For one day as he sat on his kingly behind,
as he did his king-thing *IT* popped into his mind...
Just a teeny, small thought, just a tiny to-do,
but it grew and it grew and it grew and it grew.

So he thought, "Well why not! I'm the king, am I not?
And besides, I have nothing-much better to do."

25

So he gathered together each nickel and dime,
every bright, golden, twinkling thing he could find;
Every nugget and trinket, each coin and doubloon,
and he melted and smelted from morning 'til noon.

And he fashioned an image, an idol, *a lie*,
nearly nine feet around - nearly ninety feet high!

Well he looked at that thing. And that thing looked at him.
and that big, fat king-head of his started to swim!

So he called for his pipe, and he called for his bowl,
and he called for each person he ruled or controlled.
And he lined them all up just as straight as can be,
and pronounced and proclaimed his toot-fruity decree.

"O, peoples and nations and men of all tongues!"
yelled King Nebby's yell-boy at the top of his lungs.

"When your ears hear the toots of the fifes and the flutes
and the honks of the horns and the bark of the lutes;
When harps start to plink and the band twinks to twitters
and patters and pitters their bells and their zithers,

FALL FLAT ON YOUR FACE! For the king does command,
as you crinkle and bake in the burning hot sand,
As you broil and sizzle with glee and with pleasure,
WORSHIP THIS STATUE OF NEBUCHADNEZZAR!"

And so every last person of every belief,
every doctor and lawyer and Indian chief,
Fell face-down in the sand on King Nebby's command
and they worshipped the idol he made with his hand.

"And oh yes, by the way, if you will not obey
on the day you *do not*," said the king, "you will pay!
For I've stoked up my furnace red-hotter than hot
and that's where you will go if you dare to *do-not!*"

So, as *you* might have guessed, and as most people would,
all those folks followed orders and followed them good!
Every *one* that would be, except *three* little wee...

Except three little, wee little godly good guys
with a wee-little, teeny, small, godly surprise.
Just three godly good guys who said, "NO! We won't go!"
Shadrach and Meshach and Abed-nego.

31

"Is this true?" spat King Neb. "Are you really so bol
that you three WILL NOT bow to my idol of gold?
Now let's try this again. It's quite easy. You'll see!
Simply open your mouths and repeat after me:

When your ears hear the toots of the fifes and the flutes,
and the honks of the horns and the twang of the lutes..."

"FALL FLAT ON YOUR FACE! We three heard your decree.
Your toot-fruity decree is as dumb as can be!

Do whatever you like! Do whatever you will,
throw us onto your greasy old barbecue grill!
For your burning-red, hotter than hot-as-can-be
flaming, fiery-red furnace *won't burn us*, you'll see.

For God is our God. HE IS GOD! And we vow,
if He saves us or not, WE WILL NOT EVER BOW!"

So they fired up the furnace. They made it red-hot,
seven times as red-hot as it ever had got!
And they lifted the lid and just threw them right in...

Oh, but good old King Nebby stopped dead in his tracks--
his fat tummy flip flopped - his heart melted like wax.
And his big old bug eyes popped right out of his head
when he saw what he saw... Then he gulped and he said,

"Ummm, I thought we threw *three* little godly good men
down there into the fiery, red furnace just then..."

"Oh but lookie at that... Well now, what do you know.
I see FOUR! And I think one's an *ANGEL* - OH NO!

Their ropes are un-tangled! Their clothes are un-burnt!
They're just waltzing and schmaltzing around like they weren't
ever wound-up and bound-up and frittered and fried.
GET THEM OUT, OUT OF THERE - NOW! GET THEM OUT!" the king cried.

So those three bopped on out just as cool as you please,
and King Nebby fell down on his knobby king-knees
and yelled, "Praise be to GOD! For at last I can see..."

The god that I made I made all by *myself* -
Made by money and power - by strength and by wealth.
Throw *THAT* stuff in the furnace and *it* would have burned!
Oh, but thanks to you godly, good guys I have learned.

I can not make god - oh, but God *CAN make me.*
Now *my* God will be GOD and GOD'S work will be ME!

God's second Commandment is:

2. MAKE NO GOD WITH YOUR HANDS

THE STORY OF DAVID AND GOLIATH

1 SAMUEL 17:1-50

Two armies were gathered on two distant hills,
and the army on one gave the other the chills.
But both armies were fuming and ready to fight,
and it looked like at any time now they just might!

When what to their wondering eyes did appear,
but a soldier so terrible, mean and severe
From the army of *there*, that the army of *HERE*
was french-frazzled with fear from the front to the rear.

He was biggeth and talleth and largeth and higheth,
he stretched from the ground straight on up to the sky-eth!
Yes, armed to the teeth both above and beneath;
a big, burly Philistine *giant* -

GOLIATH!

"Who wants to FIGHT?" He fee-fi foed and foo'd.
"Come on, put up your dukes! Come get blackened and blued!
I will fight for MY army! So pull up your drawers,
and send out one wee-warrior to fight me for yours!"

Well, they put up their dukes, every one - one and all,
but their dukes were all saggy and baggy and small!
So they sucked in their guts and they threw out their chests,
but that big, hairy giant just wasn't impressed.

"Get on out of my sight!" He spit-toodled and spewed.
"You're a bunch of big babies! *Your God is one too!*
For my name is GOLIATH - just look at this bod!
YOU WILL NEVER DEFEAT ME. Not you OR your God!"

So each night after night, and each day after day,
on and on went Goliath that very same way.
And for forty long days, on their side of the hill,
they just whimpered and sniveled and took it, *until...*

A *wee*-tiny fellow, so dinky and small
that you'd hardly believe he would matter at all,
Wandered into the camp and just happened to hear
all the fumm and the foo that had filled them with fear.

"Well just who does this Philistine think that he is?"
said that dinky, small dude in that big voice of his.
"He's insulting the Name of The Almighty GOD,
and he'll do it *NO MORE* - over my own wee bod!"

Well now word gets around just as quick as you please
when God's mighty, strong army gets wobbly knees,
And a dinky, small dude with a big, Godly trust
comes along and says, *"I'll do the job! Yes, I must!"*

And that's why, when King Saul, who'd been flipping his lid,
and who's knees knobbled harder than anyone's did,
Heard that dinky small Dave had been mocking *Goliath*,
said, "Hey, let's go get him and give him a try-eth!"

So the king gave young David his helmet and boots
and his shield and his sword and his giant-proof suit,
And he figured that David was ready to groove
when in fact dinky Dave was unable to move!

"*I CAN'T fight like this!* Man, I can't even *see*,
this stuff might work for YOU, but it won't work for ME!
Now, I told you before, but I'll tell you again--
It is God who will fight. It is GOD who will win!"

So wee David de-booted, disrobed and undressed
and untangled that old tin-can-tankerous mess,
Bolted down to the stream, gathered five small, smooth stones,
and took off like the wind, bent to rattle some bones!

Well, Goliath looked down just below his left knee
and then what to his wondering eyes did he see,
But a wee-teeny fellow, so dinky and small
that you'd hardly believe he could matter at all!

"What AM I, a DOG?!?" thundered mean old Goliath,
"that you send me this teeny-small, not-very-higheth
wee, peach-fuzzy pup with a stick and some rocks?
Oooh, I'm shakin' the whole way on down to my socks."

"Well then fight like a man!" rumbled dinky, small Dave.
"What's the matter, you sissy? Go on - make my day!
For this battle is GOD'S. And in GOD's mighty name,
on this day I'M the hunter and YOU are the GAME!"

And so out came his sling, and then in went a stone,
and wee, dinky, small Dave, in a way all his own
Slung it 'round and around and around and about,
and that one tiny, smooth, shiny pebble flew out.

Like a *photon-torpedo* - like *lightning* it sped,
and it bopped old Goliath right-square in the head!

"Oh my word!" said Goliath. *"That smarts!* Ooooh, that stings!
I see planets and stars and all kinds of nice things!"
Then he teetered and tottered. He pitched and he yawed...

And fell down with a *"crash!"* fat-head-first in the sod.

You can puff yourself up. It won't help you at all,
for the bigger you puff, then the harder you fall.
But when GOD is your strength, you're a hundred feet tall...

Even though you're the smallest, wee person of all.

God's third Commandment is:
3. LOVE MY NAME

In the beginning, way back at its birth,
God created the heavens and cooked-up the earth.
For without a big-bang or a pop or a fizz,
out of *nothing* at all He made all that there is!

But the earth was asleep in the darkness of night,
snuggled up - until God said, *"Now let there be light!"*
And light was! And that very first blazing, clear light
was the light of His glory, His love and His might.

And God looked at the light and He saw it was good,
it was lighting things up just the way that it should.
It just rolled up the darkness and chased it away...

There was evening and morning, the very first day.

Genesis

Then God said, "Let the waters that cover the world
be untangled, untied, opened up and unfurled.
Let them gather above, let them billow and puff
into cloudy, white, pillowy cotton and fluff.

Let them gather below - let them bubble and crash,
let them babble and gurgle and splatter and splash!

Let the sky stay up high. Let the sea stay down low,"
and that's just where they stayed, as you already know.
And as you might have guessed, and as I now know too...

There was evening and morning on day number two.

Oh, but day number *three* - it was something to see,
it was something to see back on day number three!
For on day number three God said, "Now let there be
lumpy clods of dry sod where there used to be sea!"

And so up from the gurgling, bubbling deep,
up and up from their slumbery, salty, blue sleep,
There arose mighty mountains of muddy, brown goop -
sopping soggy, wet piles of primordial soup!

And God called that goop land and the rest He called sea,
then He dried the place up just for you and for me.

Then He said, "Let My land produce veggies and fruits,
from their stems and their shoots all the way to their roots."
So that's just what they did. It was something to see,
on that evening and morning on day number three.

You say your head's spinning? Well, mine's spinning too,
with all that God's done, just what more could He do?
Oh but then, once again, as the night dropped and fled,
God unfolded the silence and silently said,

"Now let there be lights in the darkness of space,
tiny, twinkling star lights all over the place -
Glassy, golden-light spinning-white, sparkling spheres,
Let them sing out the seasons and mark out the years!"

And the sun came alive with the gift of His light,
and it shone with the light of His love and His life!
And then high in the inky blue black of the night
He ker-plopped down the moon to reflect back its light.

What a day. I should say! Could there be any more,
after morning and evening on day number four?

But on day number five the whole world came alive --
came alive and went right into wild overdrive!

"Let the waters be filled up with whales and with fish
and all manner of things that swim wiggle and swish."
And then," said the Lord, "let each salmon and tuna
in every last sea, river, lake and lagoona,

Each grunion and grunt, every grouper and crappie,
each wahoo and halibut, mammie and pappie,
Live happily, and then let every last one
have a million fish daughters and little fish sons!

Let the sky fill with cock-a-doo doodlers and peepers,
quack, hootie-hoot, tweedle humm-honkers and cheepers,
Big buntings and bitterns, macaws, and ma-quacks,
tiny, tufted, winged things from the fronts to the backs."

And God saw all the dancing and splashing and singing,
the laughter and joy that His love had been bringing.
He saw it was good. It was free and alive--
there was morning and evening on day number five.

Then on day number six God just pulled out the stops,
of all days, some would say that *this day* was the tops!
For when *this day* was through, all that God had begun,
all the work that He worked would at last be all done.

So God said, "Let the land produce creatures and critters
in waggles and gaggles and big, kitty litters.

Lions and tigers and pandas and grizzlies,
moo-milky brown cows - furry fuzzies and frizzlies
Tyrano meat-munchers - bum buzzling bees
and then every last thing in betwixt or between."

And God looked all around and He saw it was good,
every thing did its thing just the way that it should.

"So now let us make man - let us make *him* alone
in our image and likeness," said God from His throne.
"Let him love and be loved. Let him know and be known,
let him rule our creation and make it his home."

And so in His own image God made up the man,
male and female he made them, just as He had planned.
Without cavemen or monkeys or riddles or tricks…

there was evening and morning on day number six.

On day seven God rested from all He had done,
He had finished the work that His hand had begun.
And He took that one day, and he called that day blessed,
and He set it apart there from all of the rest.

So this Sunday, I think I'll plop down in my pew,
and get down on my knees and say, "Thanks!" *Wouldn't you?*

For each breath that I take - every thump of my heart
is a *gift,* and without Him I truly would not
Have one slender, slim thing. *I'd have nothing,* it's true!

Oh the depth of His love! *I'll remember* - will YOU?

God's fourth Commandment is:
4. KEEP MY SABBATH

ABRAHAM AND ISAAC

GENESIS 22:1-18

Moms and dads and dads and moms.
Yes, that's right where the trouble comes!

For moms and dads have scuffs and skids,
but moms and dads make little kids!
And little kid's dos, don'ts, and dids
make dads and moms just flip their lids!

And I should know. Oh, yes I should,
yes I should know, and know but good!
For long ago, way back before
my beard dip-doodled to the floor,

Before my skin was crimped and crinkled,
crumpled, creased, and Rip-Van Wrinkled,
back when I was just a lad -
I fell in love - *with Mom and Dad!*

Now, *my* dad was some dad. Yes, *my* dad was 'oooh-awed.'
For *my* dad was a dad who was trusting in God!
And he'd tell me how he *always* wanted a son,
and how one day God popped in and promised him one.

"I'm one-hundred years old!" Pop would say that he said.
"To have kids at MY age would be out of your head!
How on earth could it happen in this here old house,
here, with this here old grandpa, and this here old spouse?!?"

Oh, but happen it did. And that son - *it was me,*
and we three were as happy as happy could be!
And my happy, old mom and her tubby, old hubby
gave thanks for their wee, chunky, chubby bear-cubbie.

But then came that one unforgettable day -
that one weed-wacky day that just blew us away!
That ONE day when God said, "Abe, get up and away,
and go do just exactly the thing that I say..."

So we hobbled and bobbled. We clipped and we clopped
for three days in the desert, then finally we stopped.
And I'll never forget, as we stood in that place,
the mysterious, queerious look on his face,

As my dad looked at me, and so silently said...

"Son, our Father is wise, and our Father knows best.
We'll just do what He says and let Him do the rest."

Then Pop built up an alter and fixed it just right
to receive up our offering, there on that night.
For the sheep God required, I soon was to see,
oh, that sheep we would offer was going to be ME!

Pop bound up my hands and he tied up my feet,
and he laid me up there nice and ever so neat.
And he took out the knife and he raised it up high,
and he started to cry, and to cry, and to cry!

But I thought to myself, *"My dear father knows best.*
I'll just do what he says and let God do the rest."
And then *BAM* - down it came. Just as fast as can be...

"A-BRA-HAM!" God's voice thundered, from out of the trees
and the rocks and the clouds and the sand in the seas
"You have shown me your heart. Faithful servant - well done!
For you gave your most precious possession - YOUR SON!"

And then what to our wondering eyes did appear
only nine or ten feet over there from right here,
But a wee tiny sheep right where no one could stick it,
all tangled and tied in a prickly thicket.

And I thought to myself, "Our dear Father knows best!
I'll just do what *He* says. *His* way works out *the best*.

And we heard Him proclaim as we tramped out of sight…

*"Let your children be blessed. Let them prosper and be
more in number than all of the sand in the sea!
Let them live and be light. Let them shine and be free!
For you've done what I asked. YOU HAVE TRUSTED IN ME."*

God's fifth Commandment is:

5. LOVE YOUR MOM AND YOUR DAD

MY BROTHER'S KEEPER

GENESIS 4:1-12

A long time ago, in a far away place,
though you never would know by the look on their face
lived two men who were different, as different can be,
Cain and Abel - the offspring of Adam and Eve.

Cain worked the soil. He dug and he hoed.
Yes, he burrowed and furrowed. He mulched and he mowed.
And he weeded and feeded the seed he had sown
'til his garden was monstrously, miracle-grown!

Oh, but Abel was different. For Abel liked sheep.
Yes, he liked them so much he saw sheep in his sleep.
And their baahs and their bleats didn't bug him a bit.
Abel loved every woolly, wee one he could get!

So one day as he wandered and wiggled and walked through the grassy, green hills with his fluffy white flock, by the quiet still water, he paused and he stopped... and he thought, "*Oh my goodness. I almost forgot!*"

"My dear God is so good, and He's blessed me so much
with my little bo sheep-i-ly people and such.
I should bring Him a present - a thank-ewe - a kid!
So that's just what I'll do!" And that's just what he did.

But when Cain saw what Abel was able to do
with his tender, kind heart and his loving thank-ewe,
he looked down at the ground and he grumbled and stewed,
and thought, "I suppose I should give God a gift too."

So they both brought the very best gift that they could.
Abel gave his with joy. Cain just knew that he should.
Then from way up in heaven, God looked at their hearts.
And Cain knew that his gift was no gift from the start.

"Well now, why are you angry? Why grumble and stew,
when you knew," said the Lord, "what you really should do?
When you do what is right, that's My joy and delight.
But the choice is one-hundred percent up to you."

Oh, but Cain wouldn't listen. He just didn't care
about anyone any which way, anywhere!
So he tuned out God's voice. And the minute he did,
sin was waiting to get him, and get him *it did!*

So he hatched up a plan from up there in his head -
a *big*, bug-eyed, nasty, red, rotten-one, fed
by the *devil himself* - by his anger and gall -
to get rid of his brother, for once and for all!

Cain knew what he did. It was there on his hands.
It was there in his heart - on the ground - in the sand.

And the ground cried aloud for the thing Cain had done.

There was nowhere to go. There was nowhere to run.
There was nowhere to hide from the blinding, hot sun
as the sound of God's voice and each drop of red blood
thundered, "Where is your brother - and what have you done!?"

"God, I swear I don't know! God you surely must *see!*
I could not have done THAT! It could not have been me!"
And Cain lied and he lied. And way, deep down inside
all the love he once had simply gave up and *died*.

And for the rest of his life, to his very last day,
Cain just wandered and squandered his life clean away.
And his beautiful gardens dried up into dust.
In the very same way that they will and they must,

When our hearts grow so blind and so callous and cold
that they don't even notice the glittering gold
of the true heart of Jesus in every last soul,
from the youngest wee-pea to the oldest King-Cole.

God's sixth Commandment is:
6. DO NOT KILL

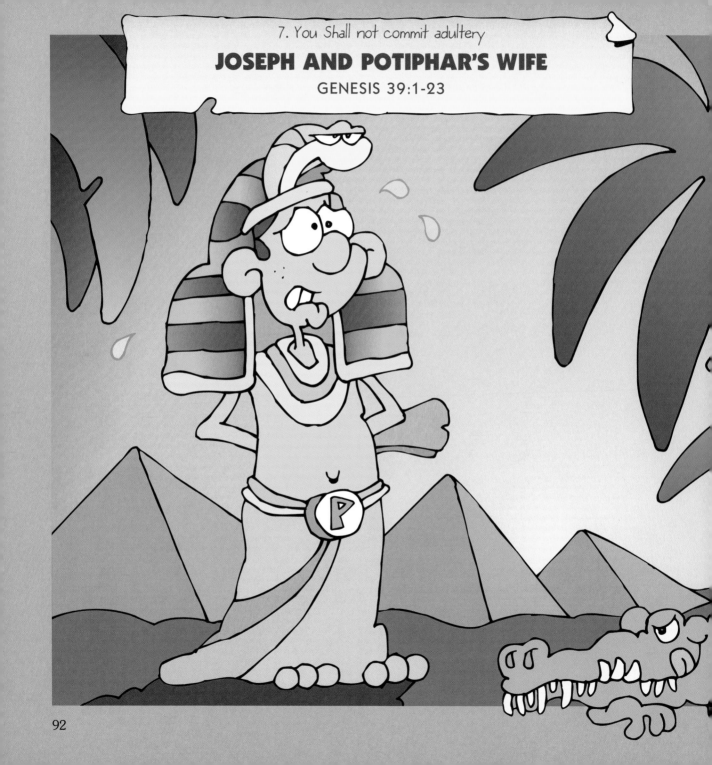

In the blazing hot sun, by the banks of the Nile,
where the sphinx never blinks, and the crocodiles smile,
just a block and a half from the Great Pyramid,
lived a man who was flipping his dusty, old lid!

For this man was in charge of each soldier and snoop
in the Pharaoh's whole gummy, green, fruit-loopy troop.
And he *did* his job well, but *his house* was a mess.
And that mess left old Potiphar dazed and distressed.

"I need some assistance," old Potiphar thought.
"And I need it right now, so I think that I ought
to go down to the market and look for a kid."
So that's just where he went. And that's just what he did!

And that wee, little slave that old Potiphar bought,
yes that wee, little slave never fussled or fought.
For wee, bitty, small Joe became Poti's best bro'.
Poti wound him on up, and oh, boy, did Joe go!

He took care of all these and all them and all those.
And he did it so well, Poti happily chose
to just go and let Joe run the whole crazy show!
And God blessed little Joe, and oh, wouldn't you know . . .

Poti never was dazed or upset or distressed.
He just put up his feet and decided to rest.
For with Joseph in charge, as I know you have guessed,
Poti's house and his gardens were all quite God-blessed.

Oh, but Joe had one tiny, small, little, wee flaw.
And that flaw was one flaw that most everyone saw!
For poor Joseph was handsome, as handsome can be.
And just what's wrong with that? Well, you surely shall see!

One day while Joe slopped with his mop and his broom,
Mrs. Poti hopped up and popped into the room.
She took one look at Joe and oh, boy, don't you know,
her brain started to go like a bad TV show!

She slithered right up to his sweet, little side
and bug-eyed him so bad that he wanted to hide.
Then she opened her mouth with a gassy, green hiss
and said, "How'z-about givin' me one little kiss?"

Joe *couldn't* believe what his ear-lobes had heard.
Mrs. Poti was naughty! Disgusting! Absurd!
But she just wouldn't stop! No she just wouldn't quit.
She was icky and yucky and that just was it!

No, I *don't* want to huggle or snuggle or smooch.
Not with you or your lipstick or even your pooch!
So please zip up your lips," little Joseph replied,
"and go take those two things back on up, and outside!"

But she *just wouldn't stop!* Every night and each day,
Mrs. Poti was naughty that very same way!
But *oh no!* Little Joe wasn't playing along.
For *his* heart was *God's* heart, and he *knew* it was wrong!

But that mean Mrs. Poti was slimy and slick.
So she cooked up a low-down, deep, dirty, old trick.
Though her outsides were pretty and really quite nice,
her poor insides were frozen-up colder than ice!

Well, she spotted wee Joe and she slid down the stairs,
and she snuggled right up to him then and right there,
then she whispered so sweet, as she wiggled her hips,
"Oh come on! Just one kiss on my big Poti-lips!"

"Oh how gross!" Joseph spat. "Go and play with your dog.
I would much rather smooch with a toad or a frog!
And just what makes you think that I *ever* would do
such a low-down deep dirty bad thing here with you?"

"For my heart is God's heart, and my kisses are too
and I'm saving them *both* for the one person who
God has chosen for ME - my sweet baby-baboo.
I don't know who it is, *but it sure isn't YOU!*"

So that mean Mrs. Poti tore off Joseph's cloak
and she ran out to find all her lawyer-type folk.
And she lied and said Joseph was trying to smooch
with her lips and her lipstick and even her pooch!

And when poor Mister Poti got wind of her tale.
He believed it and tossed little Joe right in jail!

Now I know that's not fair. And poor Joseph was used.
But what's right is what's right. And that's what we must do.
God knows where we are. And He's working it out.
And so Joe gave God thanks, and just turned right about,

And took care of all these and all them and all those
and he did it so well that the *Jailers* all chose
to just go and let Joe run the whole crazy show!

Did he ever get out? Well *he might have* - but then. . .
I'm saving that part for chapter ten!

God's seventh Commandment is:

7. GUARD YOUR HEART

ACHAN AND THE WALLS OF JERICHO
JOSHUA 5:13—7:26

You've probably heard, and may already know
about Josh and the Big Wall of Jericho - *Oh!*
How we stumbled and stomped all about and around
and the walls of that town came a' tumbling down!

But I'll bet my big toe that you never did know
or may never have heard one mysterious word
about what happened *after* the walls finally fell!
Which is what *I've* been itching to show and to tell.

We were working God's plan. We did just what He said.
Every morning at eight we all jumped out of bed
and without a wee-peep, sneaker-squeaker or sound
we marched up to the city and trotted around,

from one side to the next - through the smog and the haze,
just the way that God said, for six dusty, long days.
For *this* land was OUR land, and we knew that although
someone put up this city - it just had to go!

Then the seventh day came. We all jumped out of bed.
We knew just what to do. *We would do what God said!*
Yes, that city was ours! And it had to ker-plop.
For God said that it would - from the tip to the top.

So we stamped and we stomped and we tramped and we tromped
seven times, all around, then we suddenly stopped,
and we filled up our lungs and got ready to shout,
and watch God blow those walls straight on up and clean out.

"Now, remember," I cried, "when the walls tumble down,
we must all destroy *every last thing* in this town.
Don't pick *anything* up! Don't take *anything* home!
Not one toothbrush or Q-tip or greasy, black comb!

For God said if we snitch even *one little pot*,
He will punish us *all* - so we all better not!"

Then we all said, "AMEN!" And we started to *SHOUT!*
And the walls blew apart, both within and throughout!

Oh, but wouldn't you know, in that one certain spot,
there where *no one would know* if he did it or not -
there where no one could *see* or be seen or get caught,
Achan saw it - and TOOK IT - *and knew he should not!*

For it glittered and jingled. It twinkled and shined.
And he wanted it all! All he *ever* could find!
And he thought *he* had *IT.* But in fact it had him!
For it opened his heart and just tramped right on in,

and it tangled and choked and in-festered the place
where God once made His home - where God poured out His grace.
And what once was so rich became desperate and poor.
But he just didn't care. All he wanted was *MORE!*

So he stuffed all that stuff up inside of his shirt
and tip-toadled on back to his tent in the dirt
and he *buried* the gold and the stuff that he took
way down deeply where nobody ever would look!

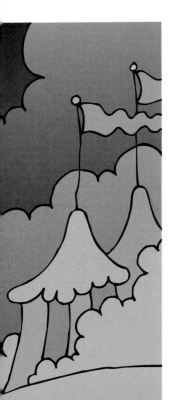

"So what's the big deal?" you may wonder today.
"Oh, it's just some old *stuff* anyhow, anyway!
No one ever will know. It will never be missed!"
But, the problem *is not* with the *stuff.* It's with this:

When *God* says DO NOT what he means is *DO NOT.*

And because of the *one* thing that Achan *DID* do,
more than thirty men died. Yes, and Achan did too!
For *God said* if they took just one pot or one lid,
He would punish them all. *So He had to - and did!*

111

God's rules are God's rules! HE IS GOD. I am not.
I will do what God *says.* For MY heart is HIS heart,
And that stays in my heart. No, it won't be forgot-

I don't need to ask why...I will simply obey.
I may not understand - *I don't have to.* Hurray!

God's eighth Commandment is:

8. DO NOT STEAL

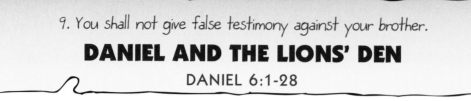

DANIEL AND THE LIONS' DEN

DANIEL 6:1-28

Well, hello there again! Getting ready for bed?
Oh, you'd like to hear one more quick story instead!
Then hold on to your bear or your beanie-bag buddy,
get comfy and snug and we'll sit back and study

the tale of a godly, good government guy -
a good, government guy *who would not cheat or lie!*
No really! It's true! Yes, he did and he was!
I'm not making it up! And I *wouldn't,* because

God requires the truth! And so Daniel was true!
Just as true as true-blue ever did or could do.

114

Daniel did his job well. In fact *he* was the best.

He was honest and truthful, wise, thoughtful and blessed.

And you'd *think* his work-mates would have loved *him* - they must!

But they *hated* his godly, good governing guts!

So those grumpy, old guys took their grouchy, old noggins
and popped out a plan to perturb and hot-dog him,
and catch him red-handed smack-dab in the act
of some low-down and dirty misdeed, but in fact . . .

though they slinked and they spied and they privately eyed
every deed Daniel did and each thing that he tried,
those two grouchy, old goobers could not find one tad,
or wee, slender, slim thing Daniel did that was bad!

Oh those grumpy, old guys were confused and perplexed!
They were popping their tops over what to do next.
When right up and on out of their angry, numb noodles
came thoughts so pitch-blackened by oodles and oodles

of years lived outside of the goodness of God
that they pestered and festered and nibbled and gnawed
at the place *in their hearts* that was faithful and true
and just chewed a big hole right on out and clean through.

"If he *will* not do something that's creepy or stinky,
We'll make something up!" they all thought, "so I think we
should wind up our wits and hum-bug a *new* plan
to get rid of that godly, good government man."

So the very next day they marched up to the king
and they smiled a big smile and then started to spring
their deceitful, dishonest despicable trick.
But the king never knew! It was over that quick.

"O great king," they sang out, all whipped-creamy and sweet,
"We bow down and we kiss your two hairy, brown feet!
For your humble, *wee* servants do wish and agree
that the king should proclaim a new royal decree . . .

that whoever would dare to give worship or praise,
or to kneel down and pray for the next thirty days
unto *anyone* other than your own sweet self
should be rounded on up from each closet and shelf

and then thrown to the lions - both damsel and dude -
to be chomped on and chewed like ferocious fast-food!"

119

"Well, that sounds good to me! Yes, that sounds like great fun.
So let's let it be written and let it be done!"
And with that the king signed a new, royal decree
that could *never* be changed - not one "q" or one "t."

Not by king or by queen. Not by damsel or dude!
Not 'till thirty long, nail-chomping days would conclude.

Well, when Daniel found out, it was truly a shock!
Oh, but what did he do? Did he shudder and knock?
Did he crawl in a hole? Did he whimper and bend?
Did he put on a mask and just try to pretend . . .

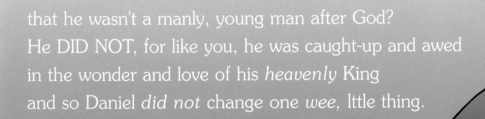

that he wasn't a manly, young man after God?
He DID NOT, for like you, he was caught-up and awed
in the wonder and love of his *heavenly* King
and so Daniel *did not* change one *wee,* lttle thing.

He went up to his room and threw open the shutters
and prayed 'til the walls and the roof and the gutters
all shook with the furious, wild love of God -
'till his heart and his mind and his chubby, wee bod

were alive with new life. Yes, he'd pray and he'd pray!
Which is just what he did at this time *every* day.

So they rounded him up like they said that they would.
Oh, those grumpy old guys thought they had him, but good!
For the king had no choice! He would *have* to conclude,
Daniel broke their new law and would have to be chewed!

But the king knew that Daniel was faithful and true.
He was true as true-blue ever did or could do!
But he made that dumb law and he knew he'd been tricked.
And so soon little Daniel'd be lapped up and licked

by those hungry, young lions - those fangs and those claws!
Oh, but what could he do? *Not one thing!* So he paused,

and said, "Throw him on in - for he flaunted his faith!
But may God whom you serve keep you comfy and safe!"
Then the king ran away to his kingly-sized bed,
and poor Daniel was thrown in and left there for dead.

And down deep in that hole with those big, hungry guys
what wee Daniel did do should have been no surprise.
For as I often say, and as everyone knows,
every cat loves to pray everywhere that he goes!

So they pulled up their rocks and their chairs and their pews
and they said their hellos and their how-do-you-dos.
And they passed the whole night - the whole godly, good time -
in Isaiah eleven, verse six through verse nine.

But the king couldn't sleep. He was up the whole night
just a tossing and turning the way that you might
if your very best friend was alone in the zoo
all because of, and on the account just of you!

So he ran to the den and tore open the door
and yelled, "Dan, are you down there?" Dan yelled back, "Oh sure!
We were just going to close with a quick word of prayer,
and then once we clean up I'll be up and right there!"

Now, as you surely know, having church the whole night
can work up a quite powerful, strong appetite.
So when Daniel walked out, guess who walked right on in...

YES, WE'RE
OPEN

We'll just leave it at that. Liars never do win.

God's ninth Commandment is:
9. DO NOT LIE

JOSEPH'S BEAUTIFUL COAT

GENESIS 37:1-47:12

Jacob had twelve handsome sons,
but *Joseph* was his favorite one -
His little baby-buckaroo.
And all his brothers knew it too!

But who could see, and who'd have thought
of all the joy and *trouble* brought
on that one tiny, tender tot,
when Jacob simply stopped and thought...

130

"I think I'll make wee Joe a coat -
a lovely coat to sport or tote.
With red and gold, with green and blue,
with purple, pink and orange, too!

The very *best* a little lad
like little Joseph ever had!"

And so he hemmed and stitched and sewed
until he thought he would explode -
until each pocket, seam and pleat
became a many-colored treat!

But oh, that coat. That colored coat!
That coat just up and got their goat!
For once Joe's brothers saw those threads,
the only thing they saw *was red!*

They'd get that coat! That coat was theirs!
Those greasy, grimy, grizzly bears
could only see that little Joe
had something they *DID NOT*, and oh,

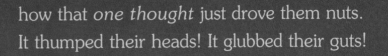

how that *one thought* just drove them nuts.
It thumped their heads! It glubbed their guts!

They had to have that techno-tweed!
That tweed they did not *even* need!
And if they could not get those threads,
they'd get poor, *little Joe* instead!

But God had plans for little Joe.
Big Godly plans! And even though
they meant to harm that little kid,
God planned to work it out - *and did!*

"C'mere you guys. Hey guys, come here!
There's something that you have to hear.
I had a dream last night in bed,
and YOU were in it!" Joseph said.

"I dreamt that we were binding wheat.
MY wheat stood up! Boy, THAT was neat.
Then YOUR wheat came and gathered round,
and bowed down 'till it touched the ground!

But wait, there's more. I've just begun.
For then the stars, the moon, the sun,
all bowed down, too. This dream was fun!
I'd say it was my favorite one!"

They screamed. They wailed. They gnashed their teeth.
Their veins popped out in disbelief!

And so those dirty, stinky guys
all snickered-up a big surprise;
a low-down, dirty-do devised
to lead to brother Joe's demise!

They grabbed his coat! They rocked his roll!
They threw him down into a hole,
a long ways down into the ground,
down where he never would be found!

"Ya' know," one greasy brother wheezed,
"this isn't right. Pop won't be pleased.
If we leave Joseph here for dead
his blood will be upon OUR head!"

"You're right!" they mumbled to each other.
"After all, he IS our brother.
Let's pull him up! Let's set him free!
Let's SELL him - INTO SLAVERY!"

Now *years* went by, as years will do,
and Jacob never, ever knew
the truth of what had happened to
his little baby-buckaroo...

A famine hit. But life went on.
Soon every scrap of food was gone!
Not one thing left to crunch or munch.
No breakfast, bedtime-snacks or lunch!

But God is *always* in control.
In fact I'd say He's on a roll!
A roll especially devised
to give those guys a BIG surprise!

For Egypt had a couple crumbs.
And any crumbly bum who'd come
would get some crumbly stuff to eat.
And so they left post-haste, toot-sweet!

They humped and bumped and thumped and lumped
across the desert, bent and slumped
and baked into a crackly crunch,
in search of something good for lunch.

But when they finally arrived
all arid, extra-hot and dried
they saw *that thing!* They saw THAT SIGHT -
that sight that filled them full of fright!

"JOSEPH!?! Who? What? Where...when, HOW?!
Oh momma-mi! Oh no! OH WOW!
Our goose is cooked!" they honked and howled.
"We're really gonna' get it now!"

His brothers gawked. They gaped. They stared.
Those guys were want-my-mommy scared!
And Joseph let them have it GOOD.
But not the way you thought he would.

"My brothers! Oh, thank God you're here!
Yes, now God's plan is crystal clear!
For as you all can plainly see,
my dream came true! *You're here with me!*

But who'd have known? Who had a clue
that God would know just what to do?

For *He* took all our dirty deeds,
our low-down, grungy grumps and greeds,
and *everything* we did or would,
and turned it all around - *for good!*

Lord, change our hearts. Please change them fast!
Oh, here we are. We're home at *last!*
Please do what only You can do.
Plow up the old. Put in the new!

The love of God.
Your dream-come-true.
Lord make it real
in my heart, too.

His brothers came and gathered round.
They bowed down 'til they touched the ground!
Yes, God had saved them ALL, but good!
And just the way He said He would.

God's Ten Commandments are:

1. I AM THE LORD

2. MAKE NO GOD WITH YOUR HANDS

3. PRAISE MY NAME

4. GO TO CHURCH

5. LOVE YOUR MOM AND YOUR DAD

6. DO NOT KILL

7. GUARD YOUR HEART

8. DO NOT STEAL

9. DO NOT LIE

10. NEVER RUN AFTER THINGS.
    RUN TO ME. YOU ARE MINE.